ACKNOWLEDGEMENTS

<u>Take Five, A Christmas Cookbook</u> is dedicated to my grandmother who taught me to love Christmas and showed me the true meaning of the season. John 3:16

Debbye Dabbs

ISBN: 0-9645899-2-3

First Printing: 1994   Third Printing: 1998
Second Printing: 1996   Fourth Printing: 200

Manufactured by
Favorite Recipes® Press
an imprint of

FRP

P.O. Box 305142
Nashville, Tennessee 37230
800-358-0560

Printed in China

TAKE FIVE COOKBOOKS

117 Muscadine Hill
Madison, Mississippi 39110

Qty		Total
_____	Take Five, A Christmas Cookbook $12.00 per book	$_____
_____	Beyond the Grill, A Cookbook for Men $12.00 per book	$_____
_____	Take Five, A Light Cookbook $12.00 per book	$_____
_____	Take Five, A Cookbook $12.00 per book	$_____
_____	Take Five A Holiday Cookbook $18.95 per book	$_____
_____	Take Five, For Every Occasion $18.95 per book	$_____
_____	Shipping and Handling $3.00 per book, includes sales tax	$_____
	Please make checks payable to Take Five Cookbooks. **Total**	$_____

Name_____

Address _____

City _____ State _____ Zip _____

Desserts

12 MENUS OF CHRISTMAS

HOT ARTICHOKE DIP

1 (14 ounce) can artichoke hearts, drained
1 cup grated parmesan cheese (fresh)
1 cup mayonnaise
⅛ teaspoon garlic salt
1 teaspoon lemon juice

Mash artichoke and add next 4 ingredients. Heat at 350 degrees for 10 minutes. Serve with wheat crackers. Yield: 10-12 servings.

 APPETIZERS • 1

CHEESE BITES

½ cup biscuit mix
1 (5 ounce) jar sharp cheese spread
3 tablespoons sesame seeds (toasted)

Mix cheese spread and biscuit mix. Shape into a ball and roll in sesame seeds. Cut into thin slices and bake on a greased cookie sheet at 375 degrees for 10 minutes. Yield: 2 dozen.

 APPETIZERS • 2

ANITA'S CHEESE BALL

1 pound grated cheddar cheese
1 cup mayonnaise
1 small onion, grated
1 cup pecans, chopped
Dash of cayenne pepper

Mix well; mold and chill. Serve with a variety of crackers. Yield:
10-12 servings.

 APPETIZERS • 3

CHRISTMAS PUNCH

2 (6 ounce) cans frozen lemonade, thawed
2 (6 ounce) cans frozen orange juice, thawed
2 (6 ounce) cans frozen limeade, thawed
2 quarts cold water
2 quarts ginger ale, chilled

Mix first four ingredients and pour over ice in punch bowl. Add ginger ale just before serving. Yield: 50 servings.

 APPETIZERS • 4

CRAB BAGEL BITES

1 small can crab meat, drained
1 (5 ounce) jar sharp cheese spread
2 teaspoons mayonnaise
¼ cup butter, melted
10 mini bagels, sliced

Combine first four ingredients. Spread on bagels. Cut into quarters. Broil 3 minutes. Yield: 40 pieces.

CAROLINE'S CHEESE TORTE

2 eggs, beaten
1 (4 ounce) can chopped green chilies
16 ounces Monterey Jack cheese, grated
2 tablespoons flour
⅓ cup milk

Mix well and pour into a greased 8 x 10 dish. Bake at 350 degrees for 35 minutes. Cool and cut into squares. Yield: 10 servings.

HOLIDAY SHRIMP MOLD

1 (8 ounce) package cream cheese, softened
1 can medium shrimp, drained
1 teaspoon mayonnaise
2 teaspoons onion flakes, dried

Mash shrimp and blend into cream cheese. Add mayonnaise and onion flakes. Place into tree or star shape mold. Chill until firm. Serve with crackers. Yield: 8-10 servings.

 APPETIZERS • 7

DEB'S TACO DIP

1 small bean dip
1 small guacamole dip
1 (8 ounce) carton sour cream
1 large jar salsa (chunky style)
2 cups grated cheddar cheese

Layer ½ of each ingredient on large plate. Repeat. Serve with chips. Yield: 12 servings.

 APPETIZERS • 8

LELIA'S RASPBERRY TEA

2 quarts water
5 teaspoons unsweetened ice tea mix
1 tub Raspberry Ice Crystal Light

Mix together and chill before serving. Yield: 16 servings.

SARA'S CHEESE STRAWS

1 teaspoon baking powder
3 cups plain flour
½ teaspoon red pepper
1 pound grated sharp cheese, room temperature
½ pound margarine (2 sticks)

Mix together. Place dough in a cookie press with a star plate. Bake on a greased cookie sheet at 400 degrees for 10 minutes. Yield: 6 dozen.

MARGARET'S MEXICORN DIP

1 cup mayonnaise
½ cup Parmesan cheese
2 cups Monterey Jack
1 can Mexicorn, drained
1 can green chilies, drained

Mix all 5 ingredients together. Bake at 350 degrees for 15 minutes or until bubbly. Yield: 6 servings.

CINNAMON SPICED CIDER

1 gallon apple cider
1 cup red cinnamon candies
1 orange, thinly sliced
2 tablespoons frozen lemonade concentrate

Combine all ingredients in a large pot. Bring to a boil. Reduce heat and simmer, uncovered, for 30 minutes. Serve hot. Yield: 16-20 servings.

LEE WILLIAMS' SHRIMP YUMMIES

1 package sliced English muffins
1 stick butter, melted
1 jar Old English cheddar cheese
1 can chopped shrimp, drained
½ teaspoon garlic salt

Mix butter, cheese, shrimp and garlic salt together. Spread on muffin halves. Cut into ¼ sections. Bake at 350 degrees for 10 minutes. Yield: 12 servings.

MEETING STREET CRAB DIP

1 (8 ounce) carton French onion dip
1 (8 ounce) package cream cheese, softened
¼ cup lemon juice
1 (7¾ ounce) can crab meat, drained

Mix first three ingredients and then add crab. Serve with crackers.
Yield: 12 servings.

 APPETIZERS • 14

BLACK BEAN DIP

2 cans black beans, drained
1 can jalapeno cheese dip
1 bunch green onions, chopped
2 tablespoons of cilantro, chopped
1 tomato, chopped

Pureé black beans in a blender. In a mixing bowl, add black beans
and remaining ingredients and mix well. Serve with tortilla chips.
Yield: 3 cups.

BRICK STREET PUNCH

4 cups hot tea
1 (24 ounce) apricot nectar
2 cups orange juice
1 small can frozen lemonade
1 (28 ounce) ginger ale, chilled

Combine hot tea, nectar, orange juice and lemonade. Chill. Add ginger ale just before serving. Yield: 1 gallon.

ASPARAGUS FOLDOVERS

2 loaves of white bread with crust removed
3 cans asparagus, drained
1 stick butter, softened
2 cups parmesan cheese, grated

Roll each bread slice flat. Spread each slice with butter and sprinkle with cheese. Place one asparagus spear on corner of bread and roll up. Secure with a toothpick. Bake for 10 minutes at 400 degrees. Yield: 30 foldovers.

LOTT LOTT'S JEZEBEL SAUCE

1 (16 ounce) jar apple jelly
1 (16 ounce) jar pineapple preserves
2 tablespoons dry mustard
1 (5 ounce) jar prepared horseradish
1 (8 ounce) package cream cheese

Mix jelly, preserves, dry mustard and horseradish. Pour over cream cheese. Serve with crackers. Yield: 4 cups.

GREEN OLIVE SPREAD

1 (8 ounce) package cream cheese, softened
½ cup mayonnaise
1 cup green olives, diced and drained (reserve juice)
½ cup pecan chips
2 teaspoons olive juice

Blend together. Serve with wheat crackers. Yield: 2 cups.

MAIN STREET CORN DIP

3 cups grated cheddar cheese
¼ cup chopped green onions
½ cup sour cream
1 (12 ounce) can Mexican style corn
½ cup mayonnaise

Mix all ingredients well. Chill. Serve with crackers or vegetables.
Yield: 3 cups.

BRASWELL MINT TEA

10 cups water
2 "family size" tea bags
1 cup sugar
1 (12 ounce) can frozen lemonade
6 sprigs mint

Boil water and mint. Add tea bags. Remove from heat. Cover for 15 minutes. Remove tea bags and mint. Add sugar and lemonade. Chill. Yield: 12 servings.

SEGREST SALAD

1 large head romaine lettuce
1 small bag frozen English peas, thawed
2 cups grated cheddar cheese
1 cup real bacon bits
1 bottle ranch salad dressing

Wash lettuce and drain. Tear into small pieces. Toss with peas, cheese and bacon bits. Pour dressing and toss before serving. Yield: 6 servings.

 SALADS • 22

SHRIMP SALAD PERDIDO

1 large lemon jello
2 cups hot water
2 cans shrimp, drained
1½ cups ketchup
1 cup diced celery

Mix all ingredients. Chill 3 hours before serving. Yield: 6 servings.

MARY'S PARTY SALAD

1 small package raspberry jello
1 cup hot water
1 can whole cranberries
1 large apple, peeled and chopped
1 cup chopped celery

Mix jello and water. Add cranberries, apple and celery. Chill for 3 hours. Yield: 6 servings.

VERY BERRY SALAD

1 (6 ounce) package raspberry jello
1 (8 ounce) package cream cheese
½ cup pecan chips
2 cans whole berry cranberry sauce
3 cups water

Boil water and add jello. Stir until jello is dissolved. Add cranberry sauce and pour into a 9 x 13 dish. Cut cream cheese into 16 squares. Form into balls and roll into pecan chips. Place in jello. Chill for 2 hours before serving. Yield: 6 servings.

FROSTY CHERRY SALAD

1 can cherry pie filling
1 large carton whipped topping
2 cups mini-marshmallows
1 large can crushed pineapple, drained
1 can sweetened condensed milk

Mix together and pour into a 9 x 13 baking dish and freeze. Take out 20 minutes before serving. Yield: 8 servings.

SKY CHIEF SALAD

1 head lettuce, cleaned and torn
1 cup mayonnaise
½ cup ketchup
⅓ cup honey
2 tablespoons lemon juice

Mix mayonnaise, ketchup, honey and lemon. Stir and serve over lettuce. Yield: 6 servings.

BROCCOLI SALAD

1 pound broccoli, washed and drained
1 pound cauliflower, washed and drained
⅔ cup mayonnaise
⅓ cup sugar
⅓ cup vinegar

Break broccoli and cauliflower into small pieces. Mix mayonnaise, sugar and vinegar. Pour over broccoli and cauliflower. Marinate overnight. Yield: 6 servings.

HOT FRUIT SALAD

3 cans chunky mixed fruits, drained
1 small jar maraschino cherries, drained
1 cup pecans, chopped
½ cup butter, melted
¾ cup brown sugar

Place fruit, cherries and pecans in a 9 x 13 casserole. Mix butter
and brown sugar. Pour over fruit. Bake at 325 degrees for 1 hour.
Yield: 10 servings.

RASPBERRY CUCUMBER SALAD

6 cucumbers, peeled and sliced
½ cup raspberry vinegar
⅔ cup sugar
½ cup vegetable oil
2 heads romaine lettuce, washed and torn

Combine cucumbers, vinegar, sugar and oil in a saucepan over low heat until warm. Place lettuce on a serving plate and top with warm sauce. Serve at once. Yield: 12 servings.

PASTA SALAD SHELTON

1 jar salad supreme seasoning spice
1 pound vermicelli, cooked and drained
3 medium fresh tomatoes, chopped
1 large onion, chopped
1 small bottle Italian salad dressing

Mix together and chill overnight. Yield: 6 servings.

KRISTEN'S SALAD

1 (8 ounce) package strawberry cream cheese, softened
1 large can crushed pineapple, drained
1 small carton non-dairy whipped topping, thawed
1 can cherry pie filling
1 cup chopped pecans

Mix cream cheese with whipped topping (use a mixer). By hand add pineapple, pie filling and nuts. Pour into 9 x 13 baking dish and freeze. Cut into squares before serving. Yield: 10 servings.

MOLDED WALDORF SALAD

2 cups apple cider
1 small package lemon jello
1 large apple, diced
¼ cup celery, chopped finely
¼ cup chopped pecans

Boil apple cider in a small saucepan and add jello. Pour mixture in an 8 x 8 casserole and chill for 30 minutes. Add remaining ingredients and chill until firm. Yield: 6 servings.

FRAN'S MONKEY BREAD

2 dozen frozen Parkerhouse rolls
1½ sticks margarine
1½ cups sugar
3 tablespoons cinnamon
1 cup chopped pecans

Thaw rolls and cut into 3 pieces. Melt margarine, add sugar and cinnamon. Dip roll into mixture. Place in an ungreased tube pan. Sprinkle nuts over layers. Let rise 2 hours. Bake 350 degrees for 40 minutes. Yield: 12 servings.

MELIA'S SAUSAGE PINWHEELS

2½ cups biscuit mix
⅔ cup cold water
1 pound of mild sausage, room temperature

Mix first two ingredients. Roll on floured surface (12 x 15). Spread sausage on top. Roll up and slice into pinwheels. Bake at 375 degrees for 12 minutes or until brown, on a greased cookie sheet. Yield: 3 dozen.

MISS DIMPLE'S CORNBREAD

1 cup self rising corn meal
½ cup sour cream
½ cup vegetable oil
2 eggs, beaten
1 large can cream corn

Mix well. Pour in greased cake pan. Bake at 425 degrees for 25 minutes. Yield: 8 servings.

FOOLPROOF CHRISTMAS BREAD

6 cups plain flour
½ cup sugar
1 stick margarine, softened
1 package yeast
2 cups warm water

Soften yeast in warm water. Add flour, sugar and margarine. Mix well. Cover and refrigerate over night. Divide dough and place in 2 greased bread pans. Let rise for 2 hours. Bake at 325 degrees for 50 minutes. Yield: 2 loaves.

JANIE'S OVERNIGHT COFFEE CAKE

1 package frozen rolls (not baked)
1 small package vanilla pudding mix (not instant)
½ cup brown sugar
½ stick melted butter
1 cup chopped pecans

Place frozen rolls in tube pan. Drizzle melted butter over frozen rolls. Mix together the dry pudding and sugar. Sprinkle over rolls. Pour melted butter over all. Add chopped nuts. Leave in oven overnight and next morning bake at 350 degrees for 45 minutes. Invert onto a plate. Yield: 12 servings.

MARY ANN'S SAUSAGE CUPS

1 can buttermilk biscuits
½ pound sausage, cooked and drained
2 cups grated Velveeta cheese

Place biscuits in a greased muffin pan to form cups. Fill with sausage and top with cheese. Bake at 400 degrees for 5 minutes. Yield: 8 servings.

REFRIGERATOR BISCUITS

1 (8 ounce) package cream cheese, softened
½ cup margarine
1 cup self-rising flour

Beat cream cheese and margarine on medium speed for 2 minutes. Add flour slowly until blended. Spoon into greased mini-muffin baking pans. Bake at 400 degrees for 15 minutes. Yield: 2 dozen.

HOLIDAY SAUSAGE WREATH

1 (16 ounce) package sausage, browned and drained
1 package refrigerated pizza dough
½ cup grated cheddar cheese

Spread pizza dough on a greased cookie sheet. Spread sausage and cheese to edges. Roll dough and shape in a ring. Bake at 350 degrees for about 20 minutes. Yield: 24 slices.

SULLIVAN BISCUITS

1 stick butter, melted
1 (8 ounce) carton sour cream
2 cups biscuit mix

Combine ingredients and blend thoroughly with fork. Drop in ungreased mini muffin tins and bake at 350 degrees for about 15 minutes. Yield: 2 dozen.

JUANITA'S CORN BREAD

3 tablespoons vegetable oil or bacon grease
2 cups self-rising corn meal mix
1½ cups buttermilk
1 egg, beaten

Mix together all ingredients and pour into a greased oven proof skillet or a 9 inch square baking pan. Bake at 425 degrees for 25 minutes. Yield: 10 servings.

MCDADE CHEESY MUFFINS

1 (16 ounce) package sausage, uncooked
1 (11 ounce) can cheese soup
½ cup water
3 cups biscuit mix

Mix together in a large bowl. Put in greased mini muffin tins and bake at 400 degrees for 15 minutes. Yield: 36.

GLEN AUBURN BLACKBERRY COFFEE CAKE

1 yellow butter cake mix
1 (8 ounce) package cream cheese, softened
½ cup oil
3 eggs
1 (15 ounce) can blackberries, drained

Mix all ingredients, except blackberries. Blend until smooth. Fold in berries. Bake in greased and floured 9 x 13 pan at 350 degrees for 40 to 45 minutes. Yield: 12 servings.

JUDY'S CORN CASSEROLE

1 can cream style corn
1 box Jiffy corn bread mix
1 small carton sour cream
½ cup oil
2 eggs, beaten

Mix ingredients. Pour into an 8 x 8 greased baking dish. Bake at 350 degrees for 30 minutes. Yield: 8 servings.

LUCAS HILL CARROTS

3 cups grated carrots, cooked and drained
1 cup mayonnaise
¼ cup butter, melted
¼ cup prepared horseradish sauce

Mix all ingredients and pour into a greased casserole dish. Bake at 350 degrees for 20 minutes. Yield: 8 servings.

ARTICHOKE AND POTATOES LADNER

3 large potatoes, baked
1 (6 ounce) jar marinated artichoke hearts, drained and chopped
2 tablespoons chopped green onions
3 tablespoons grated parmesan cheese
3 tablespoons margarine

Sauté onion and artichoke in margarine. Stir in parmesan cheese. Spoon over hot potatoes that have been cut in half. Yield: 6 servings.

FRESH MUSHROOM CASSEROLE

½ cup butter
3 (8 ounce) packages sliced fresh mushrooms
1½ cups herb-seasoned stuffing mix
2 cups shredded sharp cheddar cheese
½ cup half and half

Sauté fresh mushrooms in butter. Stir in stuffing mix. Place in 9 x 13 casserole. Top with cheese and half and half. Bake at 350 degrees for 20 minutes. Yield: 6 servings.

CASTLE CRANBERRY RELISH

2 medium oranges
1 pound cranberries
2 cups sugar
¼ cup chopped walnuts

Peel and section oranges. Reserve peel of one orange. Remove as much white membrane from the peel as possible. Grind orange sections, orange peel and cranberries using a coarse blade. Stir in sugar and nuts. Chill. Serve as meat accompaniment. Yield: 3½ cups.

PLANTER'S INN VEGETABLES

1 (16 ounce) bag frozen carrots, cauliflower and broccoli mix
1 can cream of celery soup
1 small jar diced pimentos, drained
1 cup grated cheddar cheese
1 can French fried onions

Combine thawed veggies, soup, pimento and ½ cup cheese. Pour into a 9 x 13 baking dish. Cover and bake at 350 degrees for 40 minutes. Uncover and top with remaining cheese and onions. Bake additional 5 minutes. Yield: 6 servings.

CAULIFLOWER WITH SHRIMP SAUCE

1 bag frozen cauliflower, cooked and drained
1 can cream of shrimp soup
½ cup sharp cheddar cheese, shredded

Heat soup and cheese in a saucepan. Warm to melt cheese. Place cauliflower in a serving dish and cover with soup mixture. Yield: 10 servings.

GREEN BEANS STOVALL

4 cans Blue Lake green beans, drained
2 cans artichoke hearts, drained
1½ cups sugar
1 cup olive oil
1 (8 ounce) bottle oil and vinegar salad dressing

Heat sugar, oil and salad dressing in a small saucepan. Pour over green beans and artichoke hearts. Chill overnight. Yield: 12 servings.

AMY'S CORN CASSEROLE

1 cup French onion dip
1 can French cut green beans, drained
1 can shoe peg corn, drained
1 can cream of mushroom soup
1 cup cracker crumbs

Mix first four ingredients and pour into a greased casserole. Top with cracker crumbs. Bake at 350 degrees for 45 minutes. Yield: 8 servings.

 VEGETABLES • 54

MUSHROOMS AND WILD RICE

1 box long grain and wild rice, cooked and drained
1 can cream of chicken soup
¼ cup white cooking wine
14 fresh mushrooms, sliced
2 tablespoons butter, melted

Sauté mushrooms in butter. Stir in cooked rice, soup and wine.
Yield: 8 servings.

HOLIDAY SWEET POTATOES

3 cups mashed sweet potatoes
2 eggs, beaten
1 cup sugar
1 stick butter, melted
2 cups mini marshmallows

Mix potatoes, eggs, sugar and butter. Place in a greased casserole and bake at 350 degrees for 20 minutes. Top with marshmallows and cook for 5 additional minutes. Yield: 10 servings.

AL'S GREEN BEANS

2 pounds fresh or frozen whole green beans
¾ cup chopped onions
½ cup butter (not margarine)
1 slice smoked ham, cut into cubes
3 cups water

Place onions, butter and ham in water. Boil on high for 10 minutes. Reduce heat and add green beans. Cook slowly for 15 minutes. Drain and serve. Yield: 6 servings.

CURRIED NEW POTATOES

12 new potatoes, cut in halves
4 tablespoons olive oil
½ stick butter, melted
½ teaspoon curry powder
1½ teaspoons salt

Place in 9 x 13 glass baking dish. Bake 45 minutes at 350 degrees.
Yield: 6 servings.

 VEGETABLES • 58

NANCY JONES' ASPARAGUS

2 cans asparagus spears, drained
1 can cream of mushroom soup
1 small can evaporated milk
2 cups fine egg noodles, cooked and drained
1 cup sharp cheddar cheese, grated

Mix soup and milk. Place ½ of this mixture in the bottom of a 9 x 13 casserole. Add 1 can of asparagus, ½ noodles and ½ cup cheese. Layer remaining ingredients with cheese on top. Bake at 350 degrees for 30 minutes. Yield: 8 servings.

ASPARAGUS BINFORD

1 can asparagus spears, drained
1 (2½ ounce) jar sliced mushrooms, drained
3 tablespoons butter, melted
3 tablespoons white cooking wine
½ cup fresh parmesan cheese, grated

Arrange asparagus in a 8 x 8 baking dish. Pour butter and wine over asparagus. Top with mushrooms and then cheese. Bake at 350 degrees for 15 minutes. Yield: 4 servings.

WATT'S CHRISTMAS CASSEROLE

1 pound sausage, browned and drained
5 slices of bread, cut into cubes
1 cup cheddar cheese, grated
6 eggs, beaten
2 cups milk

Place bread on bottom of a greased 9 x 13 pan. Add sausage, cheese, milk and eggs. Bake at 350 degrees for 35 minutes. Yield: 10 servings.

CHEESY GRITS

1 cup grits, cooked as directed
1 stick margarine
½ pound processed cheese
2 eggs, beaten
½ cup milk

Blend and bake in greased casserole at 325 degrees for 30 minutes. Yield: 8 servings.

MAI TAI CHICKEN WINGS

18 chicken wings, cut in half
2 cups ketchup
½ cup honey
½ cup soy sauce
½ cup lemon juice

Mix last 4 ingredients in large bowl. Place wings in marinade and chill for 12 hours. Remove and bake on cookie sheet at 275 degrees for 1 hour. Yield: 36 servings.

 MAIN DISH • 63

HAYLEY'S CHICKEN CASSEROLE

1 (24 ounce) carton sour cream
2 cans cream of chicken soup
10 chicken breasts, deboned
4 tablespoons poppy seeds
1 cup Ritz cracker crumbs

Place chicken in a 9 x 13 casserole dish. Mix sour cream, soup and poppy seeds together. Pour over chicken. Top with cracker crumbs. Bake at 350 degrees for 1 hour. Yield: 6 servings.

DR. SCOTT'S BRISKET

1 (12-16 ounce) brisket (with fat)
½ bottle liquid smoke
1 (14 ounce) bottle ketchup
2 cups brown sugar
2 tablespoons dry mustard

Mix liquid smoke, ketchup, brown sugar and mustard. Place brisket in a 9 x 13 casserole, fat side up. Pour mixture over brisket. Bake at 250 degrees for 5 hours, uncovered. Yield: 8 servings.

TURKEY ROLL-UPS

1½ cups boneless turkey
½ pound grated cheese
1 cup milk
1 can cream of chicken soup
1 can crescent dinner rolls

Mix turkey with half of cheese. Separate dinner rolls. Put 2 tablespoons turkey mixture in middle of each roll, fold like a diaper and place in greased casserole dish. Pour rest of ingredients over roll-ups. Bake at 350 degrees for 1 hour, uncovered. Yield: 4 servings.

PEARL'S CHICKEN PIE

1 small can evaporated milk
1 can cream of chicken soup
1 small can boned chicken
1 (15 ounce) can mixed vegetables, drained
2 pie crusts (folded in box)

Mix first 4 ingredients together. Pour into a 9 x 13 casserole. Place crust on top and bake at 350 degrees for 45 minutes. Yield: 6 servings.

 MAIN DISH • 67

PIZZA FLORENTINE

4 small flour tortillas
1⅓ cups frozen chopped spinach, cooked and drained
1⅓ cups mozzarella cheese, grated
1 small fresh tomato, chopped
2 teaspoons lemon-pepper

Place tortillas on a greased cookie sheet. Cover each with ⅓ cup spinach, ½ teaspoon lemon-pepper, 3 tablespoons of chopped tomato and ⅓ cup mozzarella cheese. Bake at 350 degrees for 8 minutes. Cut each tortilla into fourths. Yield: 16 servings.

DIANNE'S BAKED PASTA

1 (8 ounce) package macaroni, cooked and drained
1½ pounds hamburger meat
1 (28 ounce) jar spaghetti sauce
2 cups mozzarella cheese, grated
1 teaspoon garlic salt

Brown hamburger meat and garlic salt and drain. Add macaroni and spaghetti sauce. Pour into a 9 x 13 casserole dish. Top with cheese. Cover with foil. Bake at 350 degrees for 30 minutes. Yield: 8 servings.

 MAIN DISH • 69

ASHLEY HOUSE GRITS

3 (10¾ ounce) cans condensed chicken broth
½ cup whipping cream
1 cup quick cooking grits, uncooked
2 cups grated sharp cheddar cheese

Put broth and whipping cream in a large saucepan. Bring to a boil. Add grits. Reduce heat and simmer for 5 minutes. Add cheese and serve. Yield: 4 servings.

 MAIN DISH • 70

CORNBREAD DRESSING

4 cups chicken or turkey broth
1½ cups chopped onion
4 cups crumbled cornbread
6 cups bread or rolls, torn into pieces
6 eggs, beaten

Cook broth and onion in a small pan for 15 minutes. Mix with remaining ingredients in a large bowl. Pour in a greased 9 x 13 casserole. Bake at 400 degrees for 35 minutes. Yield: 8 servings.

BEEF POT ROAST

1 (3 pound) beef roast
1 can cream of mushroom soup
1 package dried onion soup mix

Place roast in baking dish. Cover with mushroom soup and sprinkle with dry soup mix. Cover with aluminum foil and bake at 300 degrees for 3 hours. Makes its own gravy. Yield: 6 servings.

 MAIN DISH • 72

SHRIMP TERIYAKI

2 cups fresh or frozen raw shrimp, peeled
3 tablespoons olive oil
1 cup chopped onion
1 cup chopped green pepper
1 cup teriyaki sauce or marinade

Brown onion and green pepper in olive oil. Add shrimp and cook about 5 minutes. Pour teriyaki sauce over mixture and simmer. Serve over cooked rice. Yield: 4 servings.

CHICKEN TORTILLA SOUP

1 can Rotel tomatoes and green chilies
1 family-size can chicken noodle soup
1 can white chicken
1 can chili hot beans (no substitutes)

Heat and top with grated cheddar. (Optional: Pour over tortilla chips.) Yield: 4 servings.

KAY'S HONEY-ORANGE HAM

1 (5 to 7 pound) uncooked ham
1 can frozen orange juice concentrate
1¾ cups water
¾ cup honey
1½ tablespoons cornstarch

Combine orange juice, water, honey and cornstarch in a saucepan. Cook and stir over medium heat until thickened. Place ham, fat side up, in a large baking dish. Pour ½ glaze over ham. Bake at 325 degrees uncovered for 2½ hours. Pour remaining glaze over ham and bake an additional 45 minutes. Yield: 12 servings.

MAMMY'S GIBLET GRAVY

1 turkey neck and giblets
6 cups turkey or chicken broth
3 tablespoons flour
¼ cup water
1 boiled egg, chopped

Cook turkey neck and giblets in turkey or chicken broth on low heat for 30 minutes. Remove neck and giblets from broth. Dissolve flour in ¼ cup water and add to broth. Chop giblets and add to mixture. Stir in chopped egg just before serving. Yield: 3 cups.

SHE-CRAB SOUP

6 tablespoons butter
6 tablespoons flour
1 pint half and half
¼ cup sherry
2 cans white lump crab meat

Melt butter and stir in flour. Slowly add half and half and stir until thickened. Add crab meat and stir in sherry. Yield: 6 servings.

 MAIN DISH • 77

CHRISTMAS MORNING QUICHE

1 can crescent dinner rolls
3 slices Swiss cheese
¾ cup milk (not skim milk)
3 eggs, beaten
6 slices bacon, fried and crumbled

Press dinner rolls in a 9 x 13 greased baking pan. Place cheese over dough. Add eggs and milk. Sprinkle bacon on top. Bake 425 degrees for 20 minutes. Yield: 4 servings.

 MAIN DISH • 78

TRADITIONAL TURKEY

1 (20 pound) turkey, thawed
2 tablespoons cooking oil
2 tablespoons salt
1 tablespoon pepper
1 tablespoon chopped parsley

Preheat oven to 350 degrees. Remove giblets and neck from turkey. Save these for giblet gravy. Coat turkey with oil. Sprinkle ½ salt and pepper inside the turkey. Season the outside of the turkey with remaining salt, pepper and parsley. Place turkey in a roasting pan and cover with aluminum foil. Bake for 4½ hours. Remove foil and bake for additional 15 minutes or until brown. Yield: 12 servings.

 MAIN DISH • 79

RHETTA'S GRILLED TENDERLOIN

1 cup soy sauce
¼ cup butter, melted
¼ cup lemon juice
1 teaspoon lemon pepper
2 pounds pork tenderloin

Place tenderloin in a plastic storage bag and cover with soy sauce, butter and lemon juice. Marinate overnight. Before grilling sprinkle with lemon pepper. Grill over medium coals about 12 minutes on each side. Yield: 8 servings.

ROCK CORNISH HENS

2 Rock Cornish game hens, thawed
1 cup white cooking wine
1 stick butter, melted
2 teaspoons salt
½ teaspoon tarragon

Sprinkle salt inside each hen (inside cavity). Mix butter, wine and tarragon together. Place hens in a 9 x 13 baking dish. Pour ½ of butter mixture over each hen. Bake uncovered at 350 degrees for 30 minutes. Pour remaining butter mixture over each hen and continue baking for 25 minutes. Yield: 2 servings.

LOBSTER NEWBURG

⅓ cup butter
2 tablespoons flour
2 cups whipping cream
3 cups cooked lobster meat
¼ cup white cooking wine

Melt butter over low heat and stir in flour. Gradually stir in cream.
Add lobster and white wine. Serve over dry toast. Yield: 6 servings.

CHICKEN AND STUFFING

4 large deboned chicken breasts, cooked
2 cans cream of chicken soup
1 (8 ounce) package herb-seasoned stuffing mix
½ cup butter, melted
2 cups chicken broth

Combine stuffing mix and butter. Place in a 9 x 13 casserole. Put chicken breasts on stuffing mixture. Combine chicken soup and chicken broth. Pour over chicken. Bake at 350 degrees for 40 minutes. Yield: 4 servings.

 MAIN DISH • 83

ROASTED PORK LOIN

1 (4 pound) boneless rolled pork loin
¼ cup olive oil
1 cup teriyaki marinade
¾ teaspoon minced garlic (dry)
1 tablespoon ground ginger

Combine oil, teriyaki, garlic and ginger. Remove pork halves from net. Place in a large zip-top bag and cover with marinade mixture. Refrigerate overnight. Remove pork loin and place in a greased roasting pan. Bake 325 degrees for 2 hours. Yield: 10 servings.

HARBOR TOWN FETTUCCINE

1 (16 ounce) package fettuccine, cooked and drained
⅔ cup fresh parmesan cheese, grated
½ cup butter, melted
1 cup whipping cream
1 cup sour cream

Place cooked fettuccine in a large bowl. Add next 4 ingredients and toss until fettuccine is coated. Yield: 6 servings.

 MAIN DISH • 85

TINY TACO PIES

1 (10 ounce) can biscuits
1 pound ground beef
½ cup chopped onion
1 package taco seasoning mix
1 cup sharp cheddar cheese, grated

Separate biscuit dough and slice each biscuit into 3 pieces. Place in tiny greased muffin tins. Brown meat, onion and taco mix. Place teaspoon of meat mixture on top of biscuits. Sprinkle each with cheese. Bake at 375 degrees for 8 minutes. Yield: 30 pies.

LAURIE'S CHESS SQUARES

1 box powdered sugar
1 stick butter
1 Duncan Hines yellow cake mix
1 (8 ounce) package cream cheese
4 eggs

Mix cake mix, butter and 1 egg. Press into a 9 x 13 x 2 pan. Cream sugar and cream cheese. Add remaining eggs and beat until fluffy. Pour over crust and bake at 325 degrees for 50 minutes. Cool and cut into squares. Yield: 12 servings.

SUE'S PECAN CRISPY

2 sticks margarine
1 cup brown sugar, firmly packed
1 cup chopped pecans
1 teaspoon vanilla
Graham crackers

Melt margarine; add sugar and boil for 2 minutes; cool. Add pecans and vanilla. Line cookie sheet with foil. Lay graham crackers close together. Spoon mixture onto graham crackers. Put in oven; bake for 10 or 12 minutes at 350 degrees. Cool before removing from cookie sheet. Yield: 4 dozen.

MARSHMALLOW FUDGE

½ cup margarine
1 (12 ounce) can evaporated milk
4 cups granulated sugar
1 (12 ounce) package semi-sweet chocolate chips
1 (7 ounce) jar marshmallow creme

Melt margarine in a 2 quart Dutch oven. Stir in milk and sugar. Bring to a boil, stirring constantly. Boil over medium heat until soft ball state or 238 degrees on a candy thermometer. Remove from heat and add chips, stirring until melted. Add marshmallow creme and stir. Pour into a greased 13 x 9 pan. Cool and cut into squares. Yield: 2 dozen.

JENNIE'S PEANUT BUTTER BALLS

1 (8 ounce) jar peanut butter
1½ boxes powdered sugar
½ pound margarine, softened
½ bar paraffin
2 jumbo Hershey bars

Mix peanut butter, powdered sugar and margarine. Shape into small balls. Melt paraffin and Hershey bars in a double boiler. Dip balls in melted chocolate. Place on wax paper. Yield: 72 balls.

CORNFLAKE CANDY

1 cup sugar
1 cup white Karo syrup
1 (12 ounce) jar chunky peanut butter
6 cups cornflakes

Mix sugar and Karo. Boil over medium heat and add peanut butter. Stir in cornflakes and drop on greased cookie sheet. Yield: 48 pieces.

GRANDMAMA'S PEANUT BRITTLE

1 cup sugar
¾ cup white Karo syrup
¼ cup hot water
2 cups raw peanuts
1½ teaspoons baking soda

Cook sugar, syrup and water over medium heat until boiling. Add peanuts and cook for five minutes, stirring constantly. Remove from heat and add soda. Stir an additional minute. Pour on a greased cookie sheet. Yield: 24 pieces.

SOUTHERN PRALINE CHEWS

1 box brown sugar
4 eggs
1 teaspoon vanilla
2 cups self rising flour
1 cup nuts, broken

Mix brown sugar and eggs in saucepan over low heat. Add remaining ingredients. Bake at 300 degrees for 30 minutes in a greased 9 x 13 casserole. Yield: 2 dozen.

MICROWAVE PRALINES

1 box light brown sugar
1 carton whipping cream
2 tablespoons butter
2 cups broken pecans

Stir brown sugar and whipping cream together. Microwave on high for 13 minutes. Stir in butter and pecans. Drop by spoonfuls onto aluminum foil. Cool and enjoy. Yield: 2 dozen.

KAY'S CHRISTMAS TREATS

¼ stick margarine, melted
6 cups crisp rice cereal
40 large marshmallows
2 cups chopped gumdrop candy

In a large glass bowl, place marshmallows and melted margarine. Microwave 1½ minutes. Add cereal and candy. Press into a greased 9 x 13 pan. Cool and cut. Yield: 24 servings.

COBURN PEANUT BUTTER BALLS

1 cup peanut butter
1 cup corn syrup
1¼ cups powdered sugar
1¼ cups powdered milk

Combine and roll into balls. Yield: 3 dozen.

DOUBLE "D" COOKIE BARS

½ cup margarine, melted
1½ cups graham cracker crumbs
1 (14 ounce) can sweetened condensed milk
2 cups semi-sweet chocolate chips
1 cup peanut butter chips

Pour margarine in a 9 x 13 baking pan. Sprinkle crumbs over margarine and pour milk over crumbs. Top with chips and press down firmly. Bake at 350 degrees for 25 minutes. Cool and cut into bars. Yield: 2 dozen.

SANTA'S TOFFEE

1 cup butter
1 cup sugar
1½ cups pecans
8 milk chocolate candy bars

Rub bottom of cookie sheet with butter. Sprinkle with pecans. Melt sugar with butter. Pour over nuts. Lay candy bars on top. Spread with spatula. Refrigerate. Break apart when cool. Yield: 24.

TUCK FAMILY TRUFFLES

1 jar marshmallow creme
2 tablespoons butter, melted
1 (6 ounce) package semi-sweet chocolate chips
2 cups rice crispy cereal
1 (12 ounce) package white bark coating, melted

Mix first 3 ingredients together in a large saucepan until chips are melted. Remove from heat and stir in cereal. Cool and roll into balls. Dip each ball in melted coating and place on waxed paper. Yield: 3 dozen.

RONNIE'S SURPRISE COOKIES

1 (20 ounce) package peanut butter cookie dough
1 (12 ounce) bag chocolate kisses

Take teaspoons of dough and wrap around each kiss. Place on ungreased cookie sheet. Bake at 350 degrees for 10 minutes. Yield: 3 dozen.

JUDY'S POPPY CRUNCH

3 quarts popped corn
2 cups pecan halves
1⅓ cups sugar
½ cup light corn syrup
1 cup butter

Place popped corn and pecans on a cookie sheet. Heat sugar, corn syrup and butter over medium heat for 5 minutes or 280 degrees on a candy thermometer. Pour over popped corn and pecans. Cool and break into pieces. Yield: 20 servings.

MADDREY CANDY

2 packages semi-sweet chocolate chips
¼ pound unsweetened chocolate (approximately 4 squares)
1 small can sweetened condensed milk
1 teaspoon vanilla
1 cup chopped walnuts (finely chopped)

Melt chocolates together in double boiler on low heat. Add milk. Stir and cook for about 3-5 minutes. When mixture begins to thicken, remove from heat. Add vanilla and stir. Drop by teaspoon onto wax paper. Cool. Roll into small "balls" and roll through chopped nuts. Yield: 3 dozen.

JANA'S CRANBERRY BAKE

2 cups cranberries, fresh or frozen
1 can apple pie filling
1½ cups oatmeal
½ cup brown sugar
1 stick margarine (in pats)

Layer the ingredients in the order listed above. Bake 1 hour at 300 degrees. (Optional: May be topped with chopped nuts.) Yield: 10 servings.

 DESSERTS • 103

ELEGANT DESSERT

8 lady fingers, cut in halves
½ gallon coffee flavored ice cream, softened
4 Heath candy bars, crushed
1 small container frozen non-dairy whipped topping
½ cup chocolate syrup

Line a spring form pan with lady fingers. Add ice cream and candy bars. Top with whipped topping and drizzle chocolate syrup. Freeze and serve. Yield: 8 servings.

CAPE COD FRUIT CRISP

2 (21 ounce) cans apple pie filling
1½ cups fresh or frozen (thawed) cranberries
1 cup crushed miniature cheese-filled round sandwich crackers
⅓ cup firmly packed brown sugar
3 tablespoons butter, melted

Combine cranberries and pie filling. Place in 9 x 13 casserole. Mix crackers, brown sugar and butter. Sprinkle over fruit mixture. Bake at 350 degrees for 30 minutes. Yield: 8 servings.

WILEY CARAMEL ICING

2 cups sugar
1 stick butter
1 small can evaporated milk
30 caramels, unwrapped

Bring sugar, butter and milk to a boil. Cook for 8 minutes. Add caramels and stir until caramels melt. Pour over a yellow sheet cake. Yield: 3 cups.

MERRIE'S RED VELVET CAKE

1 box yellow cake mix
4 eggs
1½ cups water
2 tablespoons cocoa
1 bottle red food coloring

Mix cake mix, eggs and water together for 3 minutes with an electric mixer. Add cocoa and food coloring and stir. Bake in 2 greased and floured 9 inch cake pans at 350 degrees for 30 minutes. Frost with Teena's Christmas Frosting. Yield: 12 servings.

TEENA'S CHRISTMAS FROSTING

1 (8 ounce) package cream cheese
½ cup sugar
½ cup confectioners sugar
1 teaspoon vanilla
1 small container frozen non-diary whipped topping, thawed

Mix well. (Great on any yellow cake!) Yield: 3 cups.

 DESSERTS • 108

AMBROSIA PUDDING

1 (11 ounce) can mandarin oranges, drained
1 (8 ounce) can pineapple tidbits, drained
4 (4 ounce) cartons vanilla pudding, already prepared
12 macaroon cookies, crushed

Combine oranges and pineapple. Layer fruit, pudding and top with cookies in parfait glasses. Yield: 4 servings.

KEY LIME PIE

1 graham cracker crumb crust
3 egg yolks
⅔ cup fresh lime juice
2 (14 ounce) cans sweetened condensed milk
1 cup whipped topping

Blend egg yolks, lime juice and condensed milk. Pour into pie shell and bake at 350 degrees for 15 minutes. Cool for 2 hours and top with whipped topping before serving. Yield: 6 servings.

FUDGE BROWNIE PIZZA

1 (10¼ ounce) package brownie mix
⅓ cup low fat yogurt (any flavor)
1 egg
1 pint chocolate ice cream, softened
1 small jar caramel ice cream topping

Mix brownie mix, yogurt and egg in a small bowl. Pour into a 9 inch greased round cake pan. Bake at 350 degrees for 25 minutes. Cool and top with soft ice cream. Freeze until firm. Serve with caramel sauce drizzled on each slice. Yield: 6 servings.

CRESS CHRISTMAS PIE

1 chocolate cookie crumb crust
2 pints cappuccino or coffee ice cream
3 ounces unsweetened chocolate squares, softened
1 can sweetened condensed milk
¼ cup milk

Fill crust with softened ice cream and freeze. Heat condensed milk, milk and chocolate over low heat. Stir until chocolate sauce is melted. Remove pie and drizzle with chocolate sauce. Yield: 6 servings.

LOW COUNTRY LEMON PIE

1 (8 ounce) package cream cheese, softened
1 (12 ounce) package non-dairy whipped topping
1 (14 ounce) can sweetened condensed milk
1 (6 ounce) can frozen lemonade, thawed
2 graham cracker crusts

Mix cream cheese, condensed milk and lemonade. Fold in whipped topping. Pour into pie crust and refrigerate for 3 hours before serving. Yield: 2 pies.

CHOCOLATE CHIP POUND CAKE

1 box Devils food cake mix
1 cup water
½ cup vegetable oil
3 eggs
½ cup chocolate chips

Combine first four ingredients and beat on low speed with mixer for 4 minutes. Fold in chocolate chips. Pour into a greased tube pan. Bake 350 degrees for 40 minutes. Yield: 12 servings.

LEMON POUND CAKE

1 (16 ounce) box powdered sugar
3 cups plain flour
1 teaspoon lemon flavoring
6 eggs
3 sticks margarine, melted

Mix ingredients together. Pour into a tube pan that has been greased and floured. Bake at 325 degrees for 1 hour. Yield: 12 servings.

 DESSERTS • 115

BLUE GRASS PECAN PIE

½ cup brown sugar
2 cups Karo syrup
½ cup butter
5 eggs, beaten
2 cups pecan halves

Heat sugar, syrup and butter over low heat about 7 minutes to dissolve sugar. Cool and add beaten eggs. Fold in pecan halves. Pour into 2 uncooked pie pastry shells. Bake at 325 degrees for 55 minutes. Yield: 2 pies.

 DESSERTS • 116

STRAWBERRY DELIGHT

1 large angel food cake, torn into small pieces
2 (10 ounce) packages frozen sweetened strawberries, thawed
¼ cup lemon juice
1 can sweetened condensed milk
1 small container frozen non-dairy whipped topping, thawed

Place cake pieces into a 9 x 13 greased casserole dish. Combine next 4 ingredients and spoon over cake. Chill 2 hours and serve. Yield: 8 servings.

 DESSERTS • 117

BLUEBERRY CRISP COBBLER

3 cups fresh or frozen blueberries
1 large can crushed pineapple
1 yellow cake mix
1 stick margarine, melted
1 cup chopped pecans

Mix first 2 ingredients. Place in a greased 9 x 13 baking dish. Sprinkle cake mix over fruit. Top with melted margarine and pecans. Bake at 350 degrees for 35 minutes. Yield: 8 servings.

12 MENUS OF CHRISTMAS

Dad's Christmas Gift
Rhetta's Grilled
Tenderloin p. 80
Curried New
Potatoes p. 58
Al's Green Beans p. 57
Ambrosia Pudding p. 109

Breakfast with Santa
Cheesy Grits p. 62
Christmas Morning
Quiche p. 78
Hot Fruit Salad p. 29
Lemon Pound Cake p. 115
Refrigerator Biscuits p. 40

Christmas Day Dinner
Traditional Turkey p. 79
Cornbread Dressing p. 71
Holiday Sweet
Potatoes p. 56
Asparagus Binford p. 60
Mary's Party Salad p. 24

Newlywed Holiday Feast
Chicken and Stuffing p. 83
Planter's Inn
Vegetables p. 51
Very Berry Salad p. 25
Foolproof Christmas
Bread p. 37

Christmas Eve Celebration
Shrimp Teriyaki p. 73
Segrest Salad p. 22
Green Beans Stovall p. 53
Cape Cod
Fruit Crisp p. 105

Trim the Tree Brunch
Cinnamon Spiced
Cider p. 12
Janie's Overnight
Coffee Cake p. 38
Watt's Christmas
Casserole p. 61
Ashley House Grits p. 70

The Kids Cook
Frosty Cherry Salad p. 26
Pearl's Chicken Pie p. 67
Christmas Punch p. 4
Fudge Brownie
Pizza p. 111

Shop 'Til You Drop
Dr. Scott's Brisket p. 65
Broccoli Salad p. 28
Judy's Corn
Casserole p. 46
Low Country Lemon
Pie p. 113

Turkey Revisited
Turkey Roll-Ups p. 66
Sky Chief Salad p. 27
Nancy Jones'
Asparagus p. 59
Key Lime Pie p. 110

Holiday Open House
Brick Street Punch p. 16
Asparagus Foldovers p. 17
Black Bean Dip p. 15
Crab Bagel Bites p. 5
Southern Praline
Chews p. 93

Carols by Candlelight
She-Crab Soup p. 77
Rock Cornish Hens p. 81
Mushrooms and
Wild Rice p. 55
Lucas Hill Carrots p. 47
Cress Christmas
Pie p. 112

Ring In the New Year
Hot Artichoke Dip p. 1
Holiday Shrimp Mold p. 7
Mai Tai Chicken
Wings p. 63
Tiny Taco Pies p. 86
Cheese Bites p. 2
Microwave Pralines p. 94

 12 MENUS OF CHRISTMAS • 120